SUN-DAY, MOON-DAY

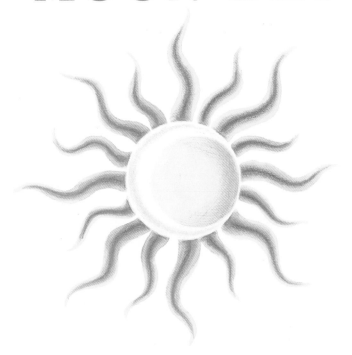

Barefoot Collections
an imprint of
Barefoot Books Ltd
PO Box 95
Kingswood
Bristol BS30 5BH
United Kingdom

First published in Great Britain and the United States in 1998 by Barefoot Books Ltd

Graphic design: Design/Section, Frome, United Kingdom
Color reproduction: Scanner Service, Verona, Italy
This book has been printed on 100% acid-free paper
Printed in Hong Kong by South Sea International Press

ISBN 1 901223 63 9

Library of Congress Cataloging-in-Publication Data is available upon request

SUN-DAY,
MOON-DAY

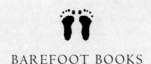

HOW THE WEEK WAS MADE

Cherry Gilchrist & Amanda Hall

BAREFOOT BOOKS

CONTENTS

Have you ever wondered why we have seven days in our week, or why some of the days have such strange names, like "Wednesday," "Friday" or "Saturday?" The story of how the week was made is a fascinating one that takes us back thousands of years into history: first to the age of the Vikings, then further back to the Romans and even further to the ancient Greeks, Egyptians and Babylonians. All these people gave something to our calendar: they found ways to measure time and the seasons, and they gave their gods and goddesses, and their stories about them, to make each day of the week different.

The week was thought to be a rather special set of seven days, ruled over by the gods of the planets. It was invented by the Babylonians, probably before 2000 BC. Later, when the Jewish stories of Creation were written down, we also find a week made up of seven days. The story of Creation that appears in Genesis, the first book of the Bible, tells us that God took seven days to create the world: six days to complete his work and a seventh day to rest and admire it.

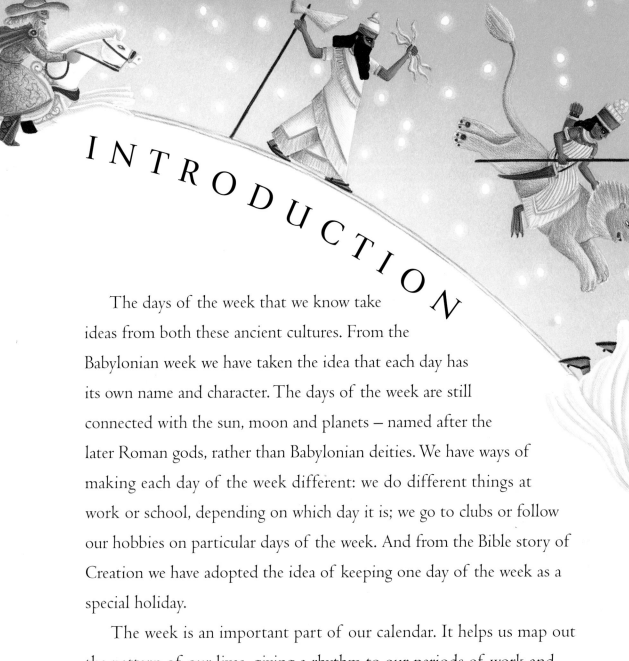

INTRODUCTION

The days of the week that we know take ideas from both these ancient cultures. From the Babylonian week we have taken the idea that each day has its own name and character. The days of the week are still connected with the sun, moon and planets – named after the later Roman gods, rather than Babylonian deities. We have ways of making each day of the week different: we do different things at work or school, depending on which day it is; we go to clubs or follow our hobbies on particular days of the week. And from the Bible story of Creation we have adopted the idea of keeping one day of the week as a special holiday.

The week is an important part of our calendar. It helps us map out the pattern of our lives, giving a rhythm to our periods of work and rest, and enabling us to record events in the past and make plans for the future. In this book you will find out more about the gods and goddesses of the week and their stories. Perhaps these tales will help to make your own week more special!

Cherry Gilchrist

Our life on earth depends upon the sun, and everywhere in the world people have always honored it. The sun god of the Aztecs was called Tezcatilipoca, or "Smoking Mirror;" he was a frightening god, and the priests offered human sacrifices to try to please him. In Japan a sun goddess named Amaterasu was worshiped. People clapped their hands to greet her in the morning, and prayed to her spirit in a special shrine. In Egypt the sun was so important that it was worshiped through several different gods: the god Aten was seen as the sun's disc, for instance, while Ra was the creator sun god who traveled across the sky in a heavenly boat.

The sun was also central to Babylonian, Greek and later to Roman culture. When the Romans became Christians in the fourth century AD, they had to choose one day of the week for worship and for rest. Both Jews and Christians share the Bible story of Creation, which tells how God created the world in six days, then made the seventh day a holy day of rest. But the Romans didn't want to copy the Jewish custom of keeping the Saturday holy, and so they finally chose

SUNDAY

Sunday. The Romans already worshiped a sun god called Mithras. And now in Christianity, the new religion, many of them saw Christ as a kind of sun god too. In AD 321, Constantine the Great made Sunday the official day of worship — and we have kept it that way ever since! It is still unusual to work on Sundays and in the past, many even considered it wicked to do so — an old English legend tells of a farmer who was swallowed up by the earth when he tried to plow his fields on Sunday.

The Greeks believed that the sun was driven across the sky in a chariot by the sun god Helios, and this story describes what happened when Helios's son, Phaethon, took charge of the chariot. The story of Phaethon seems to echo earlier legends. The Babylonians told the story of a hero called Etana, who tried to fly up to heaven on the back of an eagle, but who fell down into the sea below. Perhaps Phaethon's story is also about an eclipse of the sun. In earlier times, people were very frightened when the sun's light disappeared. They created stories to explain it, and held ceremonies to help the sun come back again.

THE CHARIOT OF THE SUN

ANCIENT GREEK

Every morning, the shining chariot of the sun rose up into the eastern sky. Up and up it soared, pulled by four winged horses, and driven by Helios, the great sun god. Higher and higher it flew. Helios stood proudly in the chariot, his golden helmet blazing and his eyes flashing with brilliant light. Soon the darkness of night had completely disappeared.

"On, on!" he cried as the chariot rose up into the highest part of the sky. The horses snorted, flame shooting from their nostrils.

At midday, the sun shone down fiercely upon the earth, and everyone could see that Helios was king of the sky again. One of the people who saw his golden chariot was a young man named Phaethon.

"That's my father," he told his friends.

"What?" they laughed. "You – the son of Helios! You're dreaming!"

Phaethon was furious. He told his mother, Clymene, how his friends teased him. "What can I do, Mother? I want to go and meet my father! How can I be sure otherwise?"

Clymene held up her arms to the bright sun.

"I swear by the light of the sun that Helios is your father! If I am lying, may I never see his light again! But if you really want to meet him, go and find him in the palace where he spends the night."

For every evening, when Helios gently reined in his tired horses, he steered his chariot down towards the western seas. Down, down it sank and the waves reflected the last red gleams of its light before it disappeared beneath them. At the far edge of the western ocean were the Islands of the Blessed, called the Hesperides. Here the chariot landed, and here Helios unharnessed his exhausted horses and gave them a magic herb to renew their strength. Then he took both chariot and horses onto a golden ferryboat that was waiting for him by the shore. While the upper earth lay in darkness, Helios and his chariot sailed back on the waters below, back to his palace in the east to rest until morning.

It was here that Phaethon found him. He had traveled a long way east to look for his father, far beyond the borders of his own country. At last he caught sight of the palace. It was the most magnificent building he had ever seen, decorated all over with shining silver and gold. Its tall pillars seemed to reach right up into the sky. Phaethon stopped in astonishment.

He wondered if he dared go in but he was not going to turn back now. He climbed up the grand staircase to the huge silver doors and walked inside. The light was so dazzling that at first Phaethon couldn't see anything.

"Who's there?" a deep voice called out.

Phaethon took a step or two forward. Now he could see that there was a throne in the center of the room, and someone on it whose face was almost too bright to look at.

"I am Phaethon," he said timidly. "I have come here to find Helios, my father."

"Phaethon!" said the figure on the throne. "Welcome! But why have you come?"

"No one will believe that you are my father!" said Phaethon. "They all laugh at me! I must know whether I am really your son or not."

Then Helios stepped down from his throne, and he took off the great crown of light so that now Phaethon could see his face.

"Yes, you are my son," he said, and he took Phaethon into his arms and hugged him. "How can I prove it to you? I'll give you anything you ask, to prove it!"

Phaethon was so dazzled by the palace, and so proud to be the son of Helios, that he didn't stop to think.

"Let me drive your chariot!" he said. "Just for one day!"

Helios was horrified. "What! Drive the chariot? Please, my dear son, ask for something different — anything but that! I'm the only person who can control those horses and keep them on the path. They are stronger than fire and wind!"

But Phaethon would not listen. If he really was the sun god's son, then he too could drive this chariot. How splendid it would be to fly right up into the sky! Everybody would see him! And no one would tease him again.

"You promised me, Father — you must let me do it!"

So, reluctantly, Helios took him out to the palace stables. The hour was close to dawn, and the horses were pawing the ground impatiently. The chariot with its golden wheels stood waiting.

"Hold on tightly to the reins!" Helios advised him. "Don't go too high, or the earth will freeze and the skies burn. Nor too low, or the earth will catch on fire and the heavens grow cold."

He helped Phaethon climb into the chariot. Then he placed the crown of light on his son's head and touched his face with a drop of magical oil for protection.

Phaethon took the reins, and in a moment the chariot was gone, flying up into the eastern sky. As it rose, day began to break upon the earth.

But this was no ordinary day. The horses galloped upwards fiercely, breathing fire, their hooves cutting through the clouds. And soon they began to swerve to right and left, which made the chariot sway dangerously. It took all Phaethon's strength to hold on to the reins.

The horses could feel that the chariot was lighter than usual. They tossed their heads, trying to snatch the reins as they raced up higher into the sky. And when Phaethon looked down, he felt sick with fright.

"Oh, what made me take my father's horses!" he thought to himself in terror. "I wish I was back on earth again! I could put up with the teasing!"

But it was too late. The horses were galloping so wildly that he could not see anything clearly. He dropped the reins in a panic.

The chariot now ran completely out of control. First it shot up towards heaven, then it suddenly dropped down low. It dropped so low that its heat began to scorch the earth itself. The fields began to smoke; the tops of the trees caught fire. Animals stampeded in terror from the blaze, people screamed and ran inside their houses, but these too began to burn. The rivers bubbled and steamed, and soon the oceans themselves boiled. It seemed that the whole earth was going to burn up. But before it was too late, Zeus, the king of the gods, took action.

"I won't let the people of the earth die like this," he said. "I won't let these creatures and forests be burnt up forever."

He took one of his deadly thunderbolts and hurled it at Phaethon. Its lightning flash struck the boy, and he fell to earth

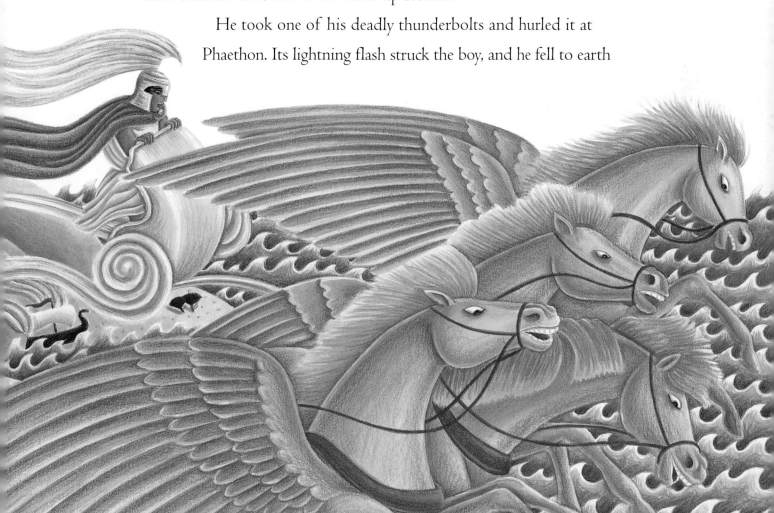

like a burning star. The chariot crashed down with him and was
smashed to pieces. The horses, mad with fear, galloped off into the
distant skies. It was a long time before anyone could catch them again.

Phaethon's body fell down from the sky into the depths of a clear,
cool river, which the heat had not yet reached. Here the god of the
river bathed him tenderly, and the nymphs of the river buried him
gently nearby.

Now the fires were out, but the disaster was not over for the earth.
Whole stretches of forests and fields were burnt up, and deserts appeared
where once there had been green grass. Great rivers were swallowed up in
the ground, and many of the trees could never bear fruit again. The earth
was changed forever.

Clymene, Phaethon's mother, was overcome with grief. She
wandered with her daughters through many lands, looking
for the place where her bright son fell to earth. At last
they found his grave by the river, and there they stayed
weeping for a long, long time. But one day Phaethon's
eldest sister found that she couldn't move anymore.

Her feet were stiff and she seemed rooted to the ground. Gradually, the same began to happen to the others. And then slowly their fingers began to change into twigs, their arms into branches and their bodies into the trunks of trees.

So it was that Phaethon's sisters became poplar trees growing on the banks of the river, still weeping for their brother. But now their teardrops were washed away by the river and turned into precious amber that was later collected and made into necklaces for brides to wear on their wedding day.

At first, when the chariot of the sun crashed to earth, everything stayed dark. Helios was also mourning for the death of his son.

"What a terrible punishment!" he said. "Why should a young man die just because he can't control those horses? I've had enough! Let somebody else drive the chariot for a change."

But when daylight never came, the people wept, and all the animals hid out of fear. Finally, the gods could bear it no longer. They came to visit Helios in his palace.

"Come back!" they said. "We must have sunlight in the world. No one can live without you, not even us!"

At last Helios agreed to put aside his grief and went out to mend the chariot, harness up the horses, and drive through the sky again every day. And every day, that is still what he does.

How often do you look at the moon? Perhaps you sometimes notice the full moon, or spot the crescent of the new moon in the night sky. But if you lived in a place where there was no electricity, you would watch the moon a lot more. You would rely on the moonlight to find your way at night. You might make journeys at the the time of the full moon, especially if you lived in a hot country. And every month, when the last thin sliver of the moon slipped back into darkness, you would wait eagerly for the next new moon. In England women used to curtsey to the new moon, and everybody would turn their money over in their pockets for luck.

Most early calendars were based on the cycles of the moon, and some still are — for instance, the Islamic calendar and the one used in southern India today. People have worshiped moon gods or goddesses from very early times.

The Chinese called their goddess of the moon Ch'ang-o. She was said to be a beautiful young woman who fled to the moon to escape from the rage of her husband, after she swallowed the Elixir of

MONDAY

Immortality that the gods had given him. The Hare
of the Moon protected her, and every year in China the
Moon Festival is still celebrated with round "mooncakes" and
family parties.

In some countries people saw the moon as a male god – the
Babylonians called their moon god Sin and believed him to be a wise
old man with a long bright blue beard and a large turban. You can meet
Sin briefly in Friday's story about the goddess Ishtar. An old English
story about the Man in the Moon states that he was sent there as a
punishment for gathering sticks on Sunday, and that you can still see
him with his bundle of sticks and his faithful dog.

The Greeks called the moon goddess Selene, though there was another
goddess, Hecate, who represented the dark phase of the moon. And the
people of old Europe saw the moon as three separate goddesses: one as
the "maiden" new moon, one as the "mother" full moon and the third as
the "old crone" dark moon. The story that follows, "The Buried Moon,"
from Lincolnshire in England, contains the traditional European idea of
the moon as a beautiful young girl.

THE BURIED MOON

OLD ENGLISH

In the marshy lands of eastern England everyone loved the moonlight. When the Moon shone at night, they could find their way through the terrible black bogs. They could keep to the safe paths and avoid the deep pools and the sucking mud that could trap you there forever. No wonder people were happy when the Moon shone, and anxious when she hid herself once a month!

And it was worse than that. When the Moon had her rest and the sky was dark, all the wicked creatures crept out of the bog. There were Bogles and Horrors and Witch Bodies and Things that you didn't have a name for and, worst of all, the Black Snag. These creatures slithered and slimed out of the bog and tried to do harm to honest folk who fell into their clutches. So, you see, nobody liked to go out when the Moon wasn't in the sky.

Now the Moon was a good, kind young maiden who wanted to keep the people of the marsh safe. And she was very upset when she heard how these awful creatures frightened them when she was not around. What could she do to help? She spent a long time worrying about this, then it occurred to her that maybe things were not quite as bad as people

20

claimed. She decided to come down to earth and have a look for herself.

So the Moon came down to earth, but nobody could see her because she was wearing her black cloak and hood. All in darkness, she stepped out into the treacherous marsh to have a look around. She could see the murky water and the black twisted stumps and the quivering grasses where no one dared to tread. She thought it was a horrible place! She trod carefully, trying to keep out of the mud. But when she heard the gurgling from the water holes and the rustling of the reeds, she began to get frightened.

Just then, she came to a big black pool, and suddenly her foot slipped! She caught at one of the tree stumps at the edge to save herself from tumbling in. But this was no ordinary stump! It was the Black Snag, and he grabbed hold of her wrists and held her in a grip as tight as steel. The poor Moon struggled and wriggled, she pushed and she pulled, but she couldn't move an inch away from the wicked Black Snag who had caught her.

Before she could think of how to escape, she heard another sound — a wailing, pitiful cry that was coming towards her. Then she heard footsteps squishing through the mud, and suddenly she saw a white face with frightened eyes staring down at her.

It was a man who had gotten lost in the marshes. He was terrified because of course the Moon was not in the sky and it was very dark. But when the Moon struggled with the Black Snag, her hood had fallen back a little, and a tiny bit of her face was showing. The man wandered towards this faint, flickering light coming from the Moon.

The Moon struggled again now because she wanted to help the man. This time her black cloak fell off completely, releasing a sudden blaze of light that shone out over the pool and the marshes. Then all the wicked creatures ran back into their holes for terror! The man shouted with joy to see the moonlight again. He was so happy that he didn't stop to see her properly, with her golden hair and shining face. He didn't think what she might be doing there, stuck in the bog with the Black Snag holding her prisoner. He just took to his heels and ran home.

And, oh, how the Moon longed to go with him! She had had quite enough of the terrible bog, and she had seen just how bad things were in the darkness. Again she fought with the Black Snag as hard as she knew how, but still he held her tightly. And at last the black hood fell back over her face and the black cloak wrapped itself around her body again and her light went out once more.

Now the evil creatures were no longer afraid of her. They came running out of their holes, sneering and jeering, calling and bawling. They spat at her, swore at her, pulled at her and pinched her. They hated her – after all, if she didn't shine so often, they could do their evil work every night.

They all crowded around the Moon, quarreling over what to do with

her, until at last the cold grey dawn began to break. Then they grabbed her with their horrible bony fingers and pushed her down into the water just below the evil Black Snag. The Bogles brought a big stone and rolled it on top of her, to stop her rising back up into the sky again. And they left two Will-o'-the-Wykes there to guard the place and mark it with their green and sickly light.

"Hooray!" all the evil creatures shouted triumphantly. "Now we can do whatever we like!"

So the poor Moon lay pinned down by a great stone, wrapped in her cloak in the cold dark water at the foot of the Black Snag. And no one knew where she was!

As the time for the New Moon came, people put pennies in their pockets ready to turn over for luck when they saw her appear. They looked out for her in the dark night sky, but the nights came and went, and the Moon never appeared. Something was wrong! The people of the marsh villages were very frightened, and some of them went together to see the Wise Woman who lived in the old mill.

The Wise Woman brought out her brewpot. She would boil it and stir it and throw herbs into it, until she could see all kinds of strange things that ordinary folk could not imagine in the bubbling liquid. She would take her mirror and gaze into it for a very long time while everybody held their breath, and then she would see things happening far away as if they

were right in front of her. Finally she
would take her book. The Wise
Woman would frown as she read it,
and scratch little signs in the ashes
on the hearth, and move her lips
as if she was counting, until at
last she had an answer. But
this time the pot did not
bubble in the right way,

the mirror showed only her own wrinkled old face, and the answers
would not come out of the book.

"It's queer," she said at last. "I can't tell you what's happened to the
Moon." The Moon was the Wise Woman's friend, and without moonlight
she found it very hard to do her magic.

So the people went away, and they talked and they argued about the
Moon, but as the days passed, still she didn't come. Then one evening, as
a group of them was sitting rather gloomily at the inn wondering what
could have happened to her, a man from another village sat up suddenly
and slapped his knee.

"Well, blow me!" he said. "I forgot all about it!"

"All about what?" they asked him.

And he told them the story of how he had been lost in the bog, and
how he had found the flickering light, and how it had blazed up like the
brightest moonlight to show him the way home.

So they went back to the Wise Woman and told her the man's story. And the Wise Woman took her brewpot and her mirror and her book again and studied them for a long time. Then she nodded her head.

"Go out just before dusk, my friends," she said, "and walk bravely right into the middle of the marsh. Keep going until you find a coffin, a candle and a cross. The Moon won't be far from there. And don't say a word, not one word, till you're home again!"

So at twilight the band of villagers set off. It was a horrible journey, stumbling and splashing through the bog, with Things whispering around their heads and fluttering against their faces. But they didn't say a word;

they just carried on until at last they

saw a huge stone lying half-submerged in the deep pool where the Moon was trapped. They stepped forward and saw the Black Snag standing just by the stone. Its twisted ugly black arms made it look just like a cross. Then they noticed a funny flickering little light, which was coming from the Will-o'-the-Wykes. The Wise Woman was right!

Now they all knelt down and said the Lord's Prayer to stop the evil creatures from harming them. But they remembered the Wise Woman's

words and said it silently to themselves, so that the Bogles could not catch them. Then they all took hold of the stone and heaved it up. Underneath it, in the water below, they saw a strange and beautiful face. And some people said afterwards that they also saw the most lovely smile on that face! But before anyone could look at her properly, a great blaze of light shone up from the pool and dazzled them. When they blinked and looked again, there was nothing there! But up in the sky now was the full Moon, as bright and beautiful and kind as ever. And the paths homeward lay before them as clear as day, and the Bogles and the wicked Things and the Witch Bodies and all the horrors of the night scampered back into their holes.

The Moon smiled down at them from above. She would have liked to send the evil creatures back into their holes forever, but even the Moon must have a rest from shining once a month.

TUESDAY

Tuesday is the day of war and is ruled by the planet Mars; hence the French and Italian words for Tuesday — *mardi* and *martedi*. In Roman times, Mars was very popular as the god of war — many battles were fought in the Roman Empire. Mars was the father of Romulus and Remus, the twins who were said to be the founders of Rome itself. In the temple of Mars in Rome, priests guarded the sacred spears and shields of the god, and for five days every spring people celebrated his festival, the Quinquatrus.

But this festival was not only for Mars; it was also the time when the goddess Minerva was worshiped. Mars and Minerva were paired together as the god and goddess of war. Whereas Mars, and the Greek god Ares before him, was a hot-tempered, quarrelsome god, Minerva was clever and cool-headed. She protected heroes, she helped Prometheus to bring fire from heaven and she captured and tamed the wild winged horse Pegasus. Minerva was known to the Greeks as Athene, the goddess of wisdom, who invented many useful things, including the chariot and the plow. Athene was born fully armed for

TUESDAY

battle, and she carried a magic shield, the aegis.

Unfortunately, there are very few stories about Mars or Ares. However, there are some very interesting stories about Minerva, which is why one of them – the story of her weaving competition with Arachne – is told here.

Nergal, the older Babylonian god of the planet Mars, is a rather shadowy figure. His symbols were the sword and the lion's head, to show his bravery. He was a war god first of all, but after he married the Queen of the Underworld, he became more important as lord of the dead and keeper of the Tablet of Wisdom.

The name "Tuesday" comes from the Norse god Tiw, but we know relatively little about him. Tiw was also a god of battle, although he was originally a god of law and government, and he had only one hand. When the gods were threatened by the giant wolf Fenrir, Tiw was brave enough to sacrifice his hand in order to capture the wolf.

Bravery, battles, hot tempers and quarrels are what Tuesday has to offer. Even Minerva, the cool warrior goddess, once flew into a rage. Read on, and find out how!

MINERVA AND ARACHNE

ROMAN

The goddess Minerva was very good at settling arguments. She had a clear head and a kind heart. Many people tried to get her help, and even the gods themselves asked her advice. Should they go to war? Who was right and who was wrong? Minerva always tried to make peace if she could. But if there was a battle, she knew better than anyone how to fight it. And if Minerva herself decided to go to war, even the gods trembled! She was fierce, brave and skillful, and no one wanted her as their enemy. But Minerva hardly ever quarreled, and only once did she lose her temper.

This is how it happened. It was not in battle, it was not in some argument with the gods or because one of the other goddesses had insulted her. It was all to do with a young girl called Arachne and Minerva's great skill as a weaver. Minerva was not only a goddess of war, but the goddess who taught women the special arts of spinning, weaving, sewing, cooking and embroidery. Everyone knew that she was the finest teacher of these arts and that they needed her help and her inspiration; everyone, that is, except Arachne.

Now, Arachne herself was an excellent weaver. She came from a

dyer's family, from a little village that was famous for making the most beautiful purple dye for wool. So Arachne grew up with spinning, dyeing and weaving going on all around her. From early on she learned how to spin the wool from a soft fleece into strong threads, how to set up a loom and how to weave cloth upon it. As she grew older, she began to weave beautiful designs in rich colors on her loom. She could embroider her cloth with wonderful pictures too, and people came from far and wide to admire her work. When the local girls heard that Arachne was finishing a new piece of cloth, they would leave their flocks or their washing by the stream or their baking in the kitchen and run up to her workshop to admire it.

"The goddess Minerva herself must be your teacher!" they said as they watched her quick and graceful fingers at work.

"No," said Arachne. "I've learned how to do all this myself — I don't need Minerva to teach me!" She laughed scornfully. The others looked at each other uneasily. It was not wise to ignore the gifts of the goddess.

Arachne bent over her work to bite off a thread. When she looked up, she saw a wrinkled, grey-haired old woman standing in front of her, leaning on a stick. She sat up in surprise. Who was this old woman? What was she doing creeping into Arachne's workshop like this?

"What do you want?" she asked rather rudely.

"Just to give you a few kind words of advice, my dear," said the old lady. "I have lost my beauty long ago – you are still young and beautiful. But other things come with age, you know, and one of them is wisdom. And so I want to warn you: be careful how you speak about a goddess like Minerva. She may hear you, and I think you should say that you are sorry. Admit that she is the finest weaver of all – then perhaps she will forgive you."

"What!" cried Arachne, jumping up. "You silly old fool! You aren't wise at all. Go and give your stupid advice to your own daughters – don't try giving it to me! If Minerva is so great, where is she? Why doesn't she appear?"

"She is here!" a voice proclaimed. Arachne watched in astonishment: gone was the old woman and in her place stood

32

the great goddess Minerva herself. She had thrown off her disguise and now appeared in all her glory. The glance from her brilliant eyes was piercing. The other girls covered their faces to protect themselves from her fierce gaze. But Arachne stared back boldly, although her heart was beating wildly.

"And now," said Minerva, "let us put this to the test. You boast that you can weave as well as I can. Come, let us see if this is true."

So the great contest began. Looms were set up, and never had two such different weavers worked in the same room – the mighty goddess Minerva and the young country girl Arachne, who thought herself as good as the goddess. Hour after hour, day after day, the work progressed. All the women of the village, and from far beyond it, came to see this extraordinary sight, creeping in and out in a hushed silence. The goddess herself was weaving at the loom! Her shuttle flew to and fro, and a shimmering rainbow of colors began to take shape upon it. People gasped when they saw the beauty of her work.

And they gasped, too, when they began to see the pictures that were growing there, for she had chosen to show the gods themselves in her cloth. Here were the twelve great deities of heaven sitting on their thrones, with Jupiter ruling over them all. Here was Neptune, god of the rivers and seas, holding his trident. Here was Minerva herself wearing full battle dress, with her helmet and spear, her famous shield with the Gorgon's head upon it dripping with serpents. Her spear pointed towards an olive tree, the tree that she had invented, her special gift to the world.

Everything in this picture was magnificent and showed how splendid
the life of the gods was. But, in each corner, Minerva wove a smaller
picture. And these pictures showed what happened to humans who
thought themselves as good as the gods: stories of how they were turned
into storks or stone steps or came to a dreadful end because of their
reckless behavior. This was certainly a message for Arachne, if she was
ready to take notice!

Meanwhile Arachne was also creating a beautiful cloth. But she chose different stories to weave — and these were stories about how the gods had tricked and cheated young girls. She showed how Jupiter had changed himself into a bull so that he could carry off the maiden Europa, and how Neptune had appeared as many creatures — a dolphin, a horse or a bird, to name but a few — so that he could come close to the young woman that he wanted and make love to her.

At last the cloths were finished, and everyone waited eagerly to see how they would be judged. Which was best? Could Arachne really weave as well as the goddess?

Minerva inspected the tapestries. To her horror, she could find no fault in Arachne's work at all. It was perfect!

And then the goddess lost her temper. She was furious! How could this ignorant girl produce work that was as good as her own? How could she match her colors so brilliantly and make her figures so real? It was too much! Arachne had insulted her, Minerva, who had invented the art of weaving, and who had taught her precious skill to these ungrateful humans. What is more, she had insulted the gods by depicting them as cheats and kidnappers!

"I will not put up with this!" she decided in a fury.

She grabbed Arachne's tapestry and ripped it in two, then she tore at it wildly until it lay in shreds on the floor. She picked up her shuttle and attacked Arachne, shrieking, like the owl that was her own bird, and hit

Arachne over and over again. Arachne could not bear the attack any longer. She had won the competition, but she could only be a loser in battle with Minerva, the goddess of war. With a heartbroken cry, she ran into the next room, out of Minerva's reach. Here she threw a rope up over a beam and tried to hang herself.

Only then, at last, did Minerva's temper melt away. Looking at Arachne, she began to feel sorry for the girl. But she was not sorry enough to let her go on living as a human being.

"You are a wicked girl!" she said. "Yet I won't let you die: you shall live, and you shall live forever, but you will hang forever too!"

So saying, she took out a bitter, magic juice and sprinkled Arachne with it. Arachne's face began to shrivel up – her hair fell off, her ears and nose too. Her body got smaller and rounder until finally she was transformed into a spider with eight thin legs and a rounded belly, hanging from her own thread.

"Now, Arachne!" said Minerva. "Hang there and spin forever! Yes, you can spin as much as you like now, and your children, and your children's children!"

And so Arachne the spider began to spin. From that day till this, she has spun her webs, and all her children know how to spin webs too, so that the world is full of spiders spinning, all because of one girl who made the goddess Minerva lose her temper.

WEDNESDAY

The gods of Wednesday are blessed with quick wits and plenty of bright ideas. Hermes, the Greek god who became the Roman Mercury, was the greatest trickster of all. On the day he was born, he stole Apollo's herd of sacred cows. He had the idea of making them walk backwards, so that no one could guess which way they had gone! A little later, he invented a marvelous new musical instrument and offered it to Apollo. The sun god was enchanted by the lyre and gave Hermes a whip to herd the cows with in exchange — he thought that putting Hermes in charge of the cows might teach him to be more responsible. But Hermes had many more tricks to play, even though he became a favorite of the gods.

The Babylonian god for Wednesday was known as Nabu. Like Hermes/Mercury, he is said to have invented the art of writing and acted as a "scribe" to the gods, writing down everything important that happened. And people treated Nabu with great respect, because he could "write" days in or out of your life to make it longer or shorter.

Hermes became the messenger of the gods, speeding through the world with wings on his heels and his helmet. He also had a more serious role,

WEDNESDAY

protecting travelers and guiding souls through the
underworld after death. And he could heal sickness. Our
most common symbol for doctors and pharmacists today is the
caduceus of Hermes, a staff with two serpents twined around it.

The name "Mercury" gives us a clue about another role played by
this god. The Latin word *mercari* means "to trade," and Mercury was the
patron saint of merchants. Julius Caesar said that Mercury was worshiped
more than any other god in Europe, which probably means that buying
and selling were very popular at the time!

It easy to see how, in Britain, the Norse god Odin took over the role
of Mercury. (Odin was also known as Woden – hence "Woden's day" or
"Wednesday," though the French and Italians keep the name "Mercury"
in their words for Wednesday – *mercredi* and *mercoledi.*) Odin, whom you
will meet in the story that follows, also liked to trick people, and meet
challenges with witty and clever solutions. He had a wild side to him,
too – he was a fierce hunter, who galloped through the sky on the wings
of the storm. But he loved art and learning, and you will see in this story
how he brought poetry itself into the world.

ODIN AND THE MAGIC MEAD

NORSE

Asgard was the land where the gods of the North lived. Here there were wonderful palaces, with roofs of silver and gold. In the great halls of these palaces, the gods feasted and drank mead, a kind of wine sweetened with honey. They guarded Asgard well, to keep the frost giants out. But men who had died bravely in battle on earth were sometimes invited to join them. They were allowed to cross the narrow rainbow bridge that led to Asgard and enter the splendid hall called Valhalla. Here they were expected to eat and drink their fill, and play noisy games. This hall was bright with the armor of soldiers, their swords flashing so brilliantly in the firelight that no other kind of light was needed there.

It is in the hall of Valhalla, where the mighty god Odin lived, that our story begins. Odin was the greatest magician, and the cleverest among the gods. But although Odin was already wise, he wanted to be wiser still. He loved wisdom so much that he had once bargained one of his eyes in exchange for a drink of water at Mimir, the spring of knowledge. He had hung upside down on the great world tree, the Yggdrasill, for nine days and nights, until magic visions came to him, and he could see everything that was happening in the world.

Odin had two helpers to bring him news from afar. These were his magic ravens, Huginn and Muninn, or "Thought" and "Memory." All night long, while the warriors and gods of Valhalla were snoring, these ravens flew over the world, gathering news to bring back to their master.

Now one morning Huginn and Muninn returned before breakfast and perched upon each of Odin's shoulders with a triumphant croak. They had a very fine story to tell, about a wonderful new kind of mead. Just one drop of it was enough to fill you with inspiration and make you a poet or a scholar. Odin was naturally most eager to have it. But there was just one problem: this mead was kept locked up by a giant called Suttungr.

This giant had a beautiful daughter named Gunnlöd. He had told her to hide the mead in a secret place and not let anyone have one drop of it. So Gunnlöd poured the mead carefully into three jugs and hid it deep inside a hollow mountain near their home.

When Odin had heard this news from his ravens, he decided to set off at once to rescue the magic mead from the giant Suttungr. He put on his broad-brimmed hat and his blue cloak. He jumped onto his horse, Sleipnir, who had eight legs and eight hooves and was the fastest horse in the world, and then he charged like a stormcloud through the sky.

At last he arrived at the land where Suttungr lived, but he knew better than to go straight to the giant's house. He rode slowly past a field where nine ugly creatures called thralls were making the hay.

When Odin saw that their scythes were very blunt, he offered to sharpen them. The thralls eagerly agreed, but once the scythes were sharp again, they all began quarreling among themselves. Soon all nine thralls were dead – hacked to death with own their newly sharpened scythes! Odin went off to tell their master, the giant Baugi, who was very upset when he heard that his nine silly thralls had killed themselves fighting each other in the fields.

Now Baugi was the brother of Suttungr, as Odin well knew. "Let me work for you this summer," he said to Baugi. "I'll do the work of nine men. All I ask in return is one drink of the magic mead that your brother Suttungr keeps hidden away."

"Well," said Baugi slowly, rubbing his beard. "I should like you to work for me, it's true. Though I don't know how I can get the mead for you. Suttungr doesn't let me anywhere near it! But if you work for me until the harvest's in, I'll come with you to Suttungr's house and see if I can help you."

And so Odin worked like nine thralls for Baugi all that summer, although Baugi didn't know who his new worker really was, for Odin called himself Bölvekr, which means "Wicked Worker."

When the harvest was in, Baugi and Odin set off for Suttungr's house.

"Brother Suttungr!" said Baugi gruffly as the two giants met.

"Brother Baugi!" replied the huge Suttungr.

"This is my loyal worker, Bölvekr," said Baugi. "He has done the work of nine thralls for me this summer. He has asked only one thing in return, and that's to have a drink of your magic mead."

"No!" roared Suttungr. "He shan't have any! No one is to have any! And don't you dare come near it, Brother, or you'll be sorry!"

Baugi and Odin did not argue, but went away again to think about what to do next.

"We'll have
to be cunning," said
Odin. "I'll decide what to
do if you will help me with
your giant's strength. Agreed?"
Baugi nodded solemnly. Odin
led him to the hollow mountain. He
could see right through the rock, and
he knew just where the mead was hidden.
Then he took out an auger, a special tool for
drilling, and handed it to Baugi. "Drill right into the
middle of the mountain," he said. Baugi started making a
hole in the rock.

"There! That's done!" he said to Odin after a while. But Odin bent
down and blew into the hole. A shower of stone dust flew back out again.

"You villain!" said Odin. "If you had really bored a hole all the way
through, the dust would fall out the other end when I blow! Now finish
the job properly!"

So Baugi, who did not much like hard work, took the auger again
and drilled all the way through to the huge, hollow chamber at the center
of the mountain.

Now Odin could really begin to use his magic. In a flash, he changed
into a serpent and darted through that hole as swift as lightning. Baugi,
jealous of Odin's magic powers, thrust the sharp auger down the hole,

trying to stab the serpent. But Odin was too quick for him. He had
already reached the inner chamber, where he now changed back into his
real shape as a god.

In front of him, her beautiful face full of surprise, stood the lovely
Gunlöd, daughter of Suttungr. Never had she seen such a
handsome, dazzling creature as this. Odin
took her hand and kissed it, and
looked long into her clear blue
eyes. He stroked her long
golden hair, and she fell
in love with him
immediately.

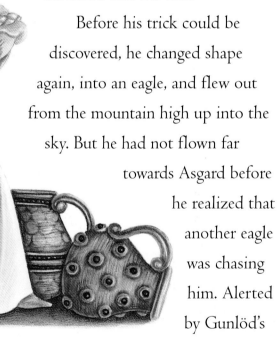

They spent three days and nights together, and then Odin asked her to give him just a few drops of the precious mead. By now, Gunlöd adored him so much that she could refuse him nothing. But she was anxious about her father, who was terrible when he was angry, and she begged Odin only to take three mouthfuls, so that Suttungr would not notice.

"One mouthful from each jug!" she told him, and brought them out from their hiding place in the rocks.

She did not know how much a god can drink. With one mouthful, Odin emptied the first jug. With another mouthful, he emptied the second, and when he lifted the third to his lips, he swallowed down every drop of the mead that was left.

Before his trick could be discovered, he changed shape again, into an eagle, and flew out from the mountain high up into the sky. But he had not flown far towards Asgard before he realized that another eagle was chasing him. Alerted by Gunlöd's

wails of grief as she saw her lover fly away, the giant Suttungr had found out that the mead was missing. He too changed into an eagle, and now his huge wings beat powerfully as he flew after the thief.

The gods saw Odin coming, Suttungr close behind him, and they ran to put out cauldrons to catch the magic liquid. Odin landed just in time, and a stream of mead poured out of his beak into the cauldrons. Now the magic mead was safe in Asgard for all time.

But when Odin was flying as an eagle, he could not keep it all in his mouth. A few drops fell out and splashed down into the world of men. Wherever one landed, so the lucky person who received it became a poet. And this was how there came to be poets among human beings. For it was the drops that fell from the Odin's beak that brought poetry into our world, and some people say that a few drops are falling still, for those who want to catch them.

The tale of Marduk's battle with Tiamat the dragon is an ancient story of Creation that comes from Babylonian times. The story tells how Marduk came to be king of the gods, and how he created the sky and stars, and the movement of time itself. Some people think that Tiamat may have been an older goddess from the earlier Sumerian period whom the Babylonians wanted to banish so that their own gods could rule the world.

The Babylonians began to chart the movements of the sun, moon and planets over four thousand years ago. They were keen mathematicians, and we still use several of their measuring systems, such as the 60-minute hour and the 360-degree circle.

The early Babylonian astronomers who studied the skies were also priests, who had to report their findings to their king. They began to develop the art that we now call astrology, which is a way of trying to understand the nature of people and events from the changing patterns in the night sky. Each night they climbed up sacred towers called ziggurats to make their observations. They worked out when to expect eclipses of the sun and moon, and predicted what these would mean — whether

THURSDAY

battles would be lost or won, whether harvests
would be good or bad.

As creator of the stars, Marduk was especially honored by
the Babylonians, and every year they held a ten-day festival for him
in which they carried his statue to a particular temple and acted out a
version of the story that follows.

The Roman god for Thursday was also the king of the gods. He
was called Jupiter, or Jove, and the Greeks knew him as Zeus. Zeus was
lord of the sky, king of the mountain peak and protector of all the
other gods. His bird was the great eagle and his tree the strong, long-
lived oak. His weapon was the thunderbolt, as poor Phaethon found
out to his dismay!

The Norse god Thor — the equivalent of Jupiter for the Vikings and
whose name has given us "Thor's day" or "Thursday" — was also famous
as a god of thunder. Whenever there was a thunderstorm, people thought
that he was driving his chariot across the skies. Thor's weapon was a
mighty hammer to protect gods and humans from the evil giants, and
also from the mighty World Serpent that lived in the depths of the sea.

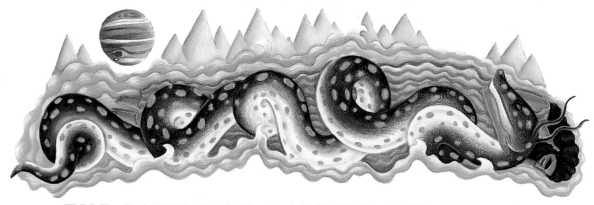

THE BATTLE OF MARDUK AND TIAMAT

BABYLONIAN

Long ago, before the world we know today came into being, there lived the first god and goddess. Tiamat was the great dragon of the deep, and her husband Apsu was the mighty lord of the fresh waters. For a long time they lived peacefully together on their own. Then they began to create new gods. After more time had passed, these gods, the children of Tiamat and Apsu, began to have children of their own.

But now there were too many gods and together they made a terrible noise! They laughed and shouted and, most of all, they liked to sing. They sang so loudly that they disturbed the sleep of Tiamat and Apsu.

Apsu could not bear it. "I can't rest!" he complained to Tiamat. "We need some sleep! We must destroy these noisy children of ours."

But Tiamat was upset at this idea. "Destroy the gods that we've created? Oh no!" she replied. "We can make them listen to us; we don't need to kill them."

Now, one of their children, Mummu, was Apsu's special messenger. And Mummu was a troublemaker. "Take no notice of Tiamat!" he told Apsu. "You must destroy the new gods you have made. You'll never have any peace otherwise!"

So Apsu started to plan his attack.

But Ea, one of the greatest of the gods, who knew everything that happened in the world, heard Apsu's words and was determined to protect the gods. So he chanted a magic spell, which floated away over the waters until it reached Apsu. The spell sent Apsu into a deep sleep, and then Ea attacked and killed both Apsu and his treacherous messenger, Mummu.

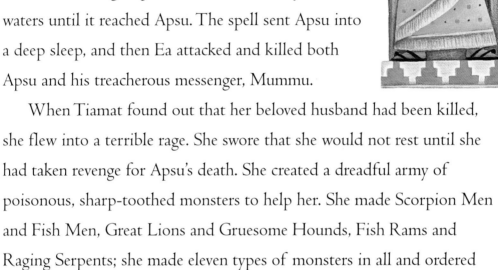

When Tiamat found out that her beloved husband had been killed, she flew into a terrible rage. She swore that she would not rest until she had taken revenge for Apsu's death. She created a dreadful army of poisonous, sharp-toothed monsters to help her. She made Scorpion Men and Fish Men, Great Lions and Gruesome Hounds, Fish Rams and Raging Serpents; she made eleven types of monsters in all and ordered Kingu, her eldest son, to be their leader.

Then Tiamat lined up her troops, admired her monsters and welcomed everyone who had decided to join her army. Now she was ready to order them all into battle. But, once again, the great god Ea heard about her plans. Ea was so shocked and angry that he could not speak for a long time. At last, when he had calmed down, he went to see his own father, Anshar, Lord of the Sky, one of the first gods that Apsu and Tiamat had created.

"What shall we do?" he asked his father. "Tiamat has created a terrible army of monsters that is ready to attack us. She has made Kingu their leader and given him the Tablets of Fate as well!"

Anshar held a meeting of all the gods and asked them what should
be done. But they just sat there, moaning in despair.

"None of us can go into battle against Tiamat," one of them said at
last. "She will kill us!"

Anshar thought deeply, and then he said, "We need the strongest
god of all to fight against Tiamat. And that is your son Marduk."

So Ea called to Marduk to come forward. When Anshar saw Marduk
standing in front of him, his heart became lighter.

"I will fight for you!" said Marduk the Brave. "Who is threatening
you? Tell me, and I will attack him!"

"It is no ordinary god – it is our mother, Tiamat, Dragon of the
Deep. She has dreadful weapons and an army of monsters. She is
planning to kill us!"

"Don't be afraid!" said Marduk. "I'll beat her!" And to the other
gods he said, "If I defeat Tiamat in battle and save your lives, then you
can make me lord of Fate, and everything I say shall come true!"

Marduk's confidence made the gods very happy, and they held a great
banquet, where they feasted on bread and sweet wine. The wine went to
their heads and they shouted and laughed again, and declared that
Marduk should be their chief god. They gave Marduk a throne and a
scepter, and a fearful ax with which to kill Tiamat.

Marduk also made himself a bow and arrow, and a net in
which to catch the dragon. He brought the winds into his power and
climbed into his storm chariot, lightning flashing all around it. His own
body was filled with fire. Drawing the chariot were four terrible beasts
called Destroyer, Merciless, Stormer and Fast Runner. They too had
sharp teeth filled with poison, and they were ready to trample and kill
anyone who stepped into their path.

Marduk galloped off, full of courage, with the gods running behind
him to see what would happen in the battle. But when Marduk came
face to face with Tiamat and Kingu and the terrible army, even he was
frightened. He hesitated. Tiamat opened her mouth to swallow him up,
and his mind became confused as he peered into her vast jaws.

The gods waited breathlessly. Then, just as the dragon was about to
swallow him whole, he recovered his courage and challenged her: "You
have made wicked trouble in the world! You are trying to rule Fate itself!
You want to destroy all the gods who were once your children! So be
ready for battle! I've come here to kill you!"

When Tiamat heard this, she became hysterical with anger, and she
trembled all over, cursing and swearing, while her troops sharpened
their weapons ready for the attack. They advanced against Marduk. But
before they could reach him, he threw the magic net over the dragon

and pulled her down. Once again, Tiamat opened her mouth, which was as big as half the world. But before she could attack him, Marduk set free one of the winds, which rushed straight inside her. Now Tiamat's belly was so swollen that she couldn't swallow anything else!

Then he took his bow and arrow, and shot her in the belly. He tied her down and stood on her till there was no more breath in her body. All the monsters ran away, and the rebel gods tried to pretend that they had never been on Tiamat's side. They wanted to come back with Marduk, but he tied them up and threw them howling into prison.

Marduk seized the Tablets of Fate from Kingu. He
put his own mark on them and hung them on his own breast.
From now on, he would be the ruler of Fate, king of the world
and of all living creatures.

The gods were cheering and shouting for joy, and they brought Marduk
presents to celebrate his victory. But he had not finished yet. He opened
the body of the great dragon and let the blood flow from her veins, to
be carried away by the north wind into the secret places of the world.

Then he cut the body of Tiamat into two, like two halves of an oyster
shell. He made the top half into the dome of heaven, and the
bottom half into the deep space that holds the earth. He

fastened the great doors of heaven tight, and he set
watchmen to guard its gates.

Next Marduk set up the stars and the planets in heaven. He
put a god to rule over each planet. He made the year and the twelve
months in it, each with its own sign of the zodiac. He set the changes
of the moon, and gave the moon a different face every seven days. Then
Marduk made sure that everything in the sky would move smoothly in its
course, and that nothing could go faster or slower than the movements of
time that he created.

And after this, the great god Marduk was ready to
create men and women to live in the world.

FRIDAY

For thousands of years in the ancient lands of Sumeria and Babylon, the story of the great goddess Ishtar was told. Later, the Greeks worshiped her as Aphrodite, then the Romans turned her into the goddess Venus. From early days the Babylonians worshiped Ishtar as the goddess of the planet Venus and of the day we call Friday. "Friday" comes from the name of the Norse goddess Friya (their equivalent of Venus), but in French and Italian you can still find the name "Venus" in their words for the day — *vendredi* and *venerdi.*

Ishtar was the Queen of Heaven and was said to be as beautiful as the starry skies. As a planet, Venus can often be seen in the evening at dusk, or early in the morning just before dawn, and to the Babylonians this was the lady Ishtar herself appearing in the skies. The Egyptians sometimes called the planet Venus "The Crosser," because it seemed to cross from east to west, from sunrise to sunset, in this way. Other ancient peoples of the east described Venus as a shining lion roaring through the heavens.

Ishtar, like Venus later, was the goddess of love. To the Babylonians, she was also the spirit of the spring, and of all growing things. Without her,

FRIDAY

there would be no love between man and woman, no baby animals, no fruit on the trees or flowers in the grass.

Ishtar herself had a lover, the young god Tammuz. He was the god of the ripe corn and the harvest, the date palm and the grapevine. When he died, she could not bear life without him, and set off in search of him in the underworld. This is the story that you will read here.

Ishtar's stories were told in the sacred temples for thousands of years, and people acted them out as dramas to bring the stories about her to life. Every year after the harvest, Babylonian women went around wailing and looking for the dead god Tammuz, and this month was named after him. When the green shoots began to appear again, they were satisfied that the god had come back to life.

Since these stories about Ishtar were told for so many years, little by little they changed. Priests and priestesses and ordinary men and women told them to their own people in their own words. What follows is just one way in which the story of Ishtar's great journey to the underworld can be told.

ISHTAR'S JOURNEY INTO THE UNDERWORLD

BABYLONIAN

Our lady Ishtar brings back the blossom to the trees. She is the one who makes the gardens green and fills the fields with barley. She is queen of the apple tree, mother of the baby lambs that skip in the new grass, and the goddess who brings love to human hearts. Her light shines in the evening sky, and the stars are a glittering girdle for her robe. Her necklaces are made of sky-blue lapis lazuli, the stones of heaven. She rides in a chariot drawn by lions, for she is swift in flight, fierce to her enemies but tender to those she loves.

Our lady Ishtar and the lord Tammuz have loved each other since the world began. He is the ripening corn that we reap, the purple grapes that we pick, the sweet dates that we feast upon. There is no one more handsome than Tammuz, no one more beautiful that the lady Ishtar.

But now a terrible thing has happened. The garden has become blackened and empty. They say our lord Tammuz is dead and the green corn will grow upon our land no more. The golden grains will never again fill our storehouses. Our lady Ishtar is in deep mourning. She is full of tears. She wails and all love is gone from her.

But Ishtar is as brave as a lion, and if Tammuz has been taken to the world below, she will go and look for him there. And so Ishtar calls her faithful friend Ninshubur, whose name means "Queen of the East." She puts on her dazzling robes, her golden ring, her necklaces and her crown. She ties on her breastplate, grasps her rod of power and opens her eyes like an owl about to enter the darkness.

Down they go, the lady Ishtar and Ninshubur. From the world above to world below, down they walk, side by side. But when they come close to the underworld, Ishtar says to Ninshubur: "Do not come with me, dear friend. Return to heaven. Tell the gods where I am, and beg them to help me. Take off your rich robes and put on a simple dress, like a poor woman. You must cry out loudly, you must make them listen. If I die here, they must send the food of life and the water of life to bring me back again."

And so Ninshubur returns to the land of the gods, and Ishtar travels

61

on until she reaches the palace of the underworld. She knocks at the gate. She speaks boldly: "Open the door, gatekeeper."

Neti, the gatekeeper, hears her voice and asks, "Who are you? Why have you come here, along the road of no return?"

"I am the Queen of Heaven, and I have come from where the sun rises. I am looking for my sister, Ereshkigal. I must speak with her."

The gatekeeper Neti leaves his place and goes to find Ereshkigal, the great Queen of the Underworld.

"Open the seven locks of the seven gates!" Ereshkigal commands Neti. "Let my sister enter!"

As Neti opens the first of the gates, he speaks to Ishtar: "Come, Lady Ishtar, you may enter. But you must take off the crown from your head and leave it here."

"What!" exclaims Ishtar. "You ask me to leave my crown behind?"

"Oh, Lady Ishtar," replies Neti, "do not question me! These are the rules of the underworld. It is for us to ask and for you to obey."

And so the lady Ishtar leaves her gleaming crown at the first gate.

At the second gate, Neti takes away her rod of lapis lazuli.

At the third gate, he takes off her necklace. At the fourth gate, off come the sparkling jewels that she wears on her breast. At the fifth gate, her golden ring is seized. At the sixth gate, her breastplate of protection is removed. At the seventh gate, she has to take off all her robes. Now the lady Ishtar, Queen of Heaven, stands naked in the darkness of the underworld.

She stands before her sister, Ereshkigal. Ereshkigal sits upon a throne with seven judges, the Anunnaki, standing at her side. Before Ishtar can beg them to release her lover, Tammuz, these seven judges turn their eyes of death towards her. They speak the word of death to our lady Ishtar. She grows pale, she becomes ill, then she dies. Now she is just a body, and Ereshkigal and the Anunnaki, the dreadful judges, hang her body on a wooden stake.

For three days, and three nights, Ninshubur waits
for Ishtar's return. Then she does as Ishtar told her.
She tears off her fine clothes and dresses in one simple
robe, like a poor woman. She runs to the gods, shrieking
and tearing her hair in grief.

First Ninshubur visits the house of the great god Enlil, he who is lord
of the hurricane and the flood.

"O Father Enlil, do not let Ishtar die in the world
below! Do not let them destroy her!"

But Enlil will not listen to Ninshubur, so she goes to
the house of Sin. Sin is the god of the moon, and some
say that he is the real father of Ishtar. Ninshubur throws
herself down before him at the foot of his throne.

"Do not let your daughter die in the underworld!" she
begs him. "She has gone there to seek the lord Tammuz! Without her the
world is growing dark and dreary! There is no love in
people's hearts anymore and the grass is parched and
brown in the fields! We cannot live without her!"

But Sin takes no notice of Ninshubur, and so, full
of sorrow, she runs to the house of Ea, father of the
waters and of the dry earth.

"Ea!" she begs him. "See my tears! They are flowing
for my lady Ishtar! Without your help she will die
forever in the world below!"

"What!" says Father Ea. "What has my daughter done now? No, life cannot continue without her. We must save her from the underworld!"

Then Ea takes the water of life and the food of life, and gives them to his own messengers to bring to Ishtar in the underworld.

When they reach the palace, Ereshkigal faces them angrily.

"She shall not leave!" she says. "Whoever enters my world below does not return!"

But the two messengers sprinkle the water of life over Ishtar and give her the food of life to eat. Ishtar's body begins to move again. Life comes into her eyes. Her face grows beautiful once more as the messengers cut her down from the post and set her on her feet.

And now Queen Ereshkigal gives a dreadful shriek, because the waters of life have been sprinkled in the world below, and the food of life eaten in the world below. Her spell over the dead has been broken. As Ishtar returns through the seven gates, she puts on her robes again, her golden ring, her necklaces and her crown. She takes up her lapis lazuli rod of power and becomes the Queen of Heaven once more. Before her run people who were once dead and are now brought back to life. They run up through the gates of death, out into the world of life.

Ishtar, Lady of Life, the lover of life, thanks her faithful friend Ninshubur. Without Ninshubur, Ishtar would still be in the house of Ereshkigal, Queen of the Dead. And so would her beloved Tammuz, the Lord of the Harvest. For when Ishtar drank of the water of life, and ate of the food of life, Tammuz was among those who were released from the underworld.

Now, in the fields that were once parched the young green corn is growing again. And now Ishtar visits Tammuz in his garden once more. They see the shoots on the grapevine, the little apples ripening on the tree and the dates growing fat on the palm. And when our lady Ishtar and our lord Tammuz love one another, we know that harvest will come again.

Our last day of the week, Saturday, is ruled by the planet Saturn, named after the Roman god. When the Romans left Britain, many of their gods were replaced with similar gods from the Norse tradition. But this was not always the case: the Anglo-Saxons called the day *Saeternesdaeg*, or "Saturn's day," and so it would appear that they kept Saturn as one of their gods.

Saturn comes from an earlier Greek god known as Cronus. Later the Greeks called him Chronos, which means "time." Saturn is also known as Old Father Time.

Old Father Time is usually pictured with a scythe, and it is said that he brings all lives to an end. People have often been afraid of him, and traditionally it was unlucky to start anything new on a Saturday. But Saturn has a good side to him too. He is the god not only of struggles and bad fortune but also of strength and deep understanding. And the Romans celebrated his festival very cheerfully. It took place in December and was called the Saturnalia. This was an occasion for much eating and drinking, and it later became our feast of Christmas.

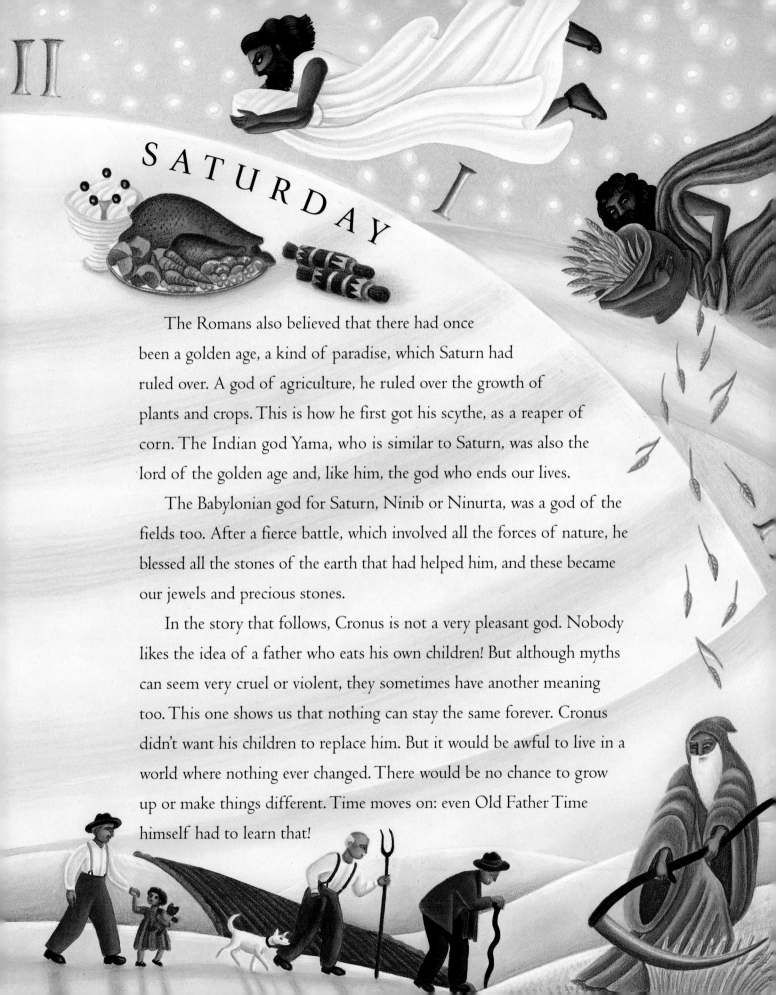

SATURDAY

The Romans also believed that there had once been a golden age, a kind of paradise, which Saturn had ruled over. A god of agriculture, he ruled over the growth of plants and crops. This is how he first got his scythe, as a reaper of corn. The Indian god Yama, who is similar to Saturn, was also the lord of the golden age and, like him, the god who ends our lives.

The Babylonian god for Saturn, Ninib or Ninurta, was a god of the fields too. After a fierce battle, which involved all the forces of nature, he blessed all the stones of the earth that had helped him, and these became our jewels and precious stones.

In the story that follows, Cronus is not a very pleasant god. Nobody likes the idea of a father who eats his own children! But although myths can seem very cruel or violent, they sometimes have another meaning too. This one shows us that nothing can stay the same forever. Cronus didn't want his children to replace him. But it would be awful to live in a world where nothing ever changed. There would be no chance to grow up or make things different. Time moves on: even Old Father Time himself had to learn that!

THE CHILDREN OF CRONUS

ANCIENT GREEK

Once, long ago, Mother Earth and Father Sky gave birth to twelve children. They were giants and they were called the Titans. The youngest of the Titans was named Cronus, and in time he became the ruler of the whole world. He married his sister Rhea, and as more time passed, they began to have children together.

But each time a baby was born, Cronus was terrified. His own parents, Gaia, mother of the deep earth, and Uranus, father of the starry sky, had warned him that one of his children would take his place as ruler of the world. Cronus could not bear the thought of this. He watched and waited, and each time a child was born he was determined that it should not live. He would take each new baby from Rhea and swallow it whole! First he swallowed their three baby girls, Hestia, Demeter and Hera, and then he swallowed his two sons, Hades and Poseidon.

Rhea was desperately unhappy and longed to have a child that would live. She wept and raged and pleaded with Cronus, but he took no notice of her. He was determined that not one of their children should grow up and threaten his kingdom. So Rhea decided to trick him and save the next baby. But how could she do this?

There was only one person she could turn to. When the baby was ready to be born, she went to see her own mother, Gaia.

"Help me! Please help me to save this child!" she pleaded. "If I don't do something, Cronus will destroy all my children, and they will never walk in this world and bring their laughter and strength to it. Everything will become old and withered and in the end the world itself will shrivel like a dying leaf."

"I will help you," Gaia replied. "I will hide the baby deep inside my body, deep inside the earth. Cronus will never find him there!"

When Rhea gave birth to a son called Zeus, Gaia quickly wrapped up her new grandchild and carried him away to the island of Crete. Here she hid him in a deep, deep cave, where no one could see or find him. Meanwhile Rhea took great care that Cronus should not get  suspicious. She chose a large stone and bundled it up in cloths, so that it looked just the right size for a baby. Then she presented the stone proudly to Cronus, pretending that this was their baby son.

"See, Cronus!" she said. "Look at our little child! Isn't he beautiful? Surely you don't want to swallow this one! Please let him live!" So she begged him and trembled as if she was terrified.

Cronus did not even bother to look at the bundle. He simply grasped it with his huge hands, and before she could say another word, he pushed it into his vast mouth and swallowed it whole. Rhea did not let her triumph show. She wept and raged as before to stop him guessing anything of her plan. But in her heart she rejoiced.

Back on the island of Crete, baby Zeus lay happy and gurgling in his cradle. When the first danger was over, he was brought out from the cave into the fresh air. Three nymphs had been chosen to care for him, and they hung his golden cradle on a tree whose shade kept the strong rays of the sun off his little face. They gave him a ball made of golden hoops to play with and looked after him as if he was their own brother. One of the nymphs, Amaltheia, could turn herself into a goat, and she gave Zeus her milk to drink to make him strong and healthy. As he began to need other food, the other two nymphs, who were the daughters of Melisseus, the honey god, commanded the bees of the mountain to bring him their scented honey to eat.

The tree where his cradle hung was in a thick forest, in a very lonely part of the island. The nymphs followed Gaia's commands and kept him there so that no strangers would see him and tell Cronus that his son was still alive. But just to make quite sure that he was safe, a group of warriors called the Curetes had been brought to his open-air nursery. They danced around his cradle all day long, beating their shields and shouting loudly so that no one could hear him crying.

As Zeus grew bigger he began to explore the mountainside around

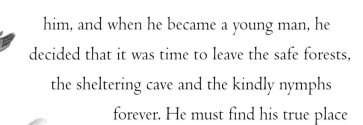

him, and when he became a young man, he decided that it was time to leave the safe forests, the sheltering cave and the kindly nymphs forever. He must find his true place in the world. First he visited Metis, a giantess who was the daughter of another Titan called Oceanus. Oceanus was lord of the stream that ran around the whole of the earth, and Metis lived beside this stream.

"Tell me what to do," Zeus said to her. "I am the son of Cronus, a Titan like your father. But it is time that his power over the world came to an end. And I must rescue my brothers and sisters too, the gods and goddesses who must rule with me in the new world."

Metis thought. "First you must go to your mother, Rhea," she said. "Ask her to smuggle you into Cronus's court and make you his cupbearer. I will give you a special drink to pour into his cup. Then wait and see what happens!"

She gave young Zeus a flask, warning him not to drink it himself and not to spill a drop until he was ready to pour it into Cronus' cup.

Zeus set off on the journey back to his mother Rhea. She was overjoyed to see him and ready to help him with his plan.

"Cronus will never recognize you!" she said. "He does not even know that you are alive! And you have grown so tall and strong. So present yourself boldly before him!"

Zeus poured the potion from the flask into the royal cup that Rhea gave him, mixing it with the honey drink that Cronus was so fond of. And then he presented it to his father as though he was just a humble cupbearer.

Cronus seized the cup and swallowed its contents in one gulp. In a few seconds the drink began to do its work. Cronus clutched at his

stomach, opened his enormous
mouth and began to retch violently. But
to everyone's astonishment, out of his mouth
suddenly flew the children of Rhea and Cronus. One
by one they shot out: Hestia, Demeter and Hera, the
growing goddesses, and Hades and Poseidon, the young gods!

"Now we can defeat the tyrant, our father!" they cried joyfully.
"Banish him, Zeus, our brother!"

And by this time, Zeus was so powerful and so strong that he had
no trouble in forcing old Cronus to leave his throne. Cronus had become
weak, and the time for him to rule the world was over. Now it was the
turn of the great god Zeus, leading the new gods and goddesses, to rule
the world in his father's place.

No one knows quite where Zeus banished Cronus. Some people
say that he was sent to the end of the earth to live there forever, quite
content but away from the changing times of this world. Others say
that he was sent to live on an island in the very west of Britain,

guarded by a race called the Hundred-
handed Ones.

Zeus did not forget the nymphs who had looked
after him so kindly on Crete. He honored Amaltheia,
the goat nymph, by putting her picture among the stars in
the sky. She became the starry constellation of Capricorn, the
sign of the goat. And to the daughters of Melisseus, the honey
god, he gave a magic horn that was always full of food and drink,
whatever kind they wished for. This was called the Cornucopia or
Horn of Plenty.

And so the world began to change and grow, and life began to take
shape, and now the old days of the Titans have nearly been forgotten. But
we still remember Cronus by his later name of Saturn, and we keep his
day as Saturday, the seventh day of the week. We think of him especially
as Old Father Time, who reminds us that one day everything comes to an
end. And with the day of Saturn our week comes to an end too, though
there is always a new one waiting to begin.

DID YOU KNOW THAT...?

THE ROMANS GOT INTO A BIG MESS WITH THEIR CALENDAR?

By the time Julius Caesar was Emperor of Rome, the calendar was in a terrible mess – it just didn't add up! The officials tried to vary the length of the year, making it between 355 and 378 days long, or adding an extra month. But often the seasons were so far off that Floralia, the Festival of Spring, didn't happen until the summer!

Julius Caesar decided to straighten all this out. He called to his court the best experts in mathematics, astronomy and even philosophy and asked them what to do. Finally, a wise man called Sosigenes from Alexandria worked out a way of making the calendar right. So Caesar ordered that from 1 January AD 45, every year was to be 365 days long, with an extra day added in every fourth year. This was the beginning of what we know as a leap year.

OUR CALENDAR IS KNOWN AS THE GREGORIAN CALENDAR?

But the Julian Calendar did not quite match up with the real length of the solar year. In 1582, Pope Gregory introduced a new calendar into Europe that adjusted the leap years a little so that time ran more smoothly. But only Catholic countries that followed the Pope took up the Gregorian Calendar. Protestant England refused to adopt it until 1752, and by then everything was eleven days off. To catch up, they had to cut out eleven days. People were so upset by this that they rioted in the streets, shouting, "Give us back our eleven days!" They thought that it had shortened their lives!

YOU CAN TELL YOUR FORTUNE FROM THE DAYS OF THE WEEK?

Maybe you already know how the rhyme about the day of the week that you were born on:

Monday's child is fair of face,
Tuesday's child is full of grace,
Wednesday's child is full of woe,
Thursday's child has far to go,
Friday's child is loving and giving,
Saturday's child works hard for a living,
But the child that is born on the Sabbath day
Is both bonny and blithe and good and gay.

But did you also know that sneezing can bring you good or bad luck, depending on the day of the week?

Sneeze on Monday – you get a letter,
Sneeze on Tuesday – you get something better,
Sneeze on Wednesday – you sneeze for danger,
Sneeze on a Thursday – meet a stranger,
Sneeze on Friday – sneeze for sorrow,
Sneeze on Saturday – see your best friend tomorrow!

MONDAY USED TO BE WASHING DAY?

Traditionally Monday was the family washday. And in the days before washing machines, it took a very long time to get clothes and sheets dried, mended, ironed and aired before the following weekend. An old rhyme scolded lazy washers:

> *If you wash on Monday*
> *You've all the week to dry.*
> *If you wash on Tuesday*
> *You've let a day go by.*
> *If you wash on Wednesday*
> *There's half the week away.*
> *If you wash on Thursday*
> *You choose an awkward day.*
> *If you wash on Friday*
> *It is because you need.*
> *If you wash on Saturday*
> *You are a slut indeed!*

GETTING MARRIED WAS ALSO RULED BY THE DAYS OF THE WEEK?

> *Monday for health,*
> *Tuesday for wealth,*
> *Wednesday the best day of all.*
> *Thursday for crosses,*
> *Friday for losses,*
> *Saturday no luck at all.*

This is what people in England once believed, when they chose a day to get married. But in other countries there were different ideas. The Italians were very gloomy about their chances of getting married on any day of the week except Sunday. "Marry on Monday," they said, "and you are sure to go mad." Danish people liked Thursdays, but the Germans avoided Thursdays, for they said it would bring "thunder" to the marriage (the German word for Thursday being *Donnerstag*, "day of thunder")!

THERE ARE MANY DIFFERENT KINDS OF CALENDARS?

The Aztecs had a four-week month, but each week was only five days long. They had names for the first day of each week: Rabbit, House, Flint and Cane. The Egyptians, on the other hand, had a much longer week of ten days. Imagine going to school for that long!

The most complicated calendar is probably the Balinese one, which has two calendars running at once. One of them, the Wuku year, has ten types of weeks. But the weeks are all of different lengths and all run at the same time. This means that each day has ten different names. The system is so hard to understand that only the priests are certain what date it is!

THERE ARE DIFFERENT KINDS OF DAYS?

The normal, twenty-four-hour day we use is called a solar day, the time it takes for the earth to turn on its axis, as measured against the sun. But there is also a sidereal day, or star day, which is measured against the background of stars and is about four minutes shorter. The sidereal day is mostly used by astronomers. There is also a lunar day, or moon day, by which we can time the high and low tides at sea.

DAYS OF THE WEEK

English	French	Italian	German	Anglo-Saxon
Sunday	dimanche	domenica	Sonntag	Sunnandaeg
Monday	lundi	lunedi	Montag	Monandaeg
Tuesday	mardi	martedi	Dienstag	Tiwesdaeg
Wednesday	mercredi	mercoledi	Wohnstag	Wodneesdaeg
Thursday	jeudi	giovedi	Donnerstag	Thuresdaeg
Friday	vendredi	venerdi	Freitag	Frigedaeg
Saturday	samedi	sabato	Samstag	Saeternesdaeg

Most of the French and Italian names for the days of the week are close to the Roman names for the gods and planets. The English and German names are closer to those of the Norse gods. Tiw's name was "Things" in Old German, which is how Tuesday becomes Dienstag; and Donner means thunder, so that Thursday is the "day of thunder" – the mark of the great god Thor.

DEITIES OF THE WEEK

Day	Planet	Babylonian	Greek	Roman	Norse
Sunday	Sun	Shamash	Helios or Apollo	Mithras	Sunna
Monday	Moon	Sin	Selene or Artemis	Diana	Sinhtgunt
Tuesday	Mars	Nergal	Ares	Mars	Tiw
Wednesday	Mercury	Nabu	Hermes	Mercury	Woden/ Odin
Thursday	Jupiter	Marduk	Zeus	Jupiter	Thor
Friday	Venus	Ishtar	Aphrodite	Venus	Friya
Saturday	Saturn	Ninurta/ Ninib	Cronus	Saturn	(Saturn)

BAREFOOT BOOKS publishes high-quality picture books for
children of all ages and specializes in the work of artists and writers from
many cultures. If you have enjoyed this book and would like to receive a copy of
our current catalogue, please contact our London office — tel: 011 44 171 704 6492
fax: 011 44 171 359 5798   email: sales@barefoot-books.com
website: www.barefoot-books.com